Legends of the Sea

Sea Monsters

Catherine Veitch

www.raintreepublishers.co.uk
Visit our website to find out
more information about
Raintree books.

To order:
☎ Phone 0845 6044371
🖹 Fax +44 (0) 1865 312263
🖥 Email myorders@raintreepublishers.co.uk

Customers from outside the UK please telephone +44 1865 312262

Raintree is an imprint of Capstone Global Library Limited,
a company incorporated in England and Wales having its
registered office at 7 Pilgrim Street, London, EC4V 6LB
– Registered company number: 6695582

Text © Capstone Global Library Limited
First published in hardback in 2010
Paperback edition first published in 2011
The moral rights of the proprietor have been asserted.

Edited by Rebecca Rissman, Nancy Dickmann,
and Siân Smith
Designed by Joanna Hinton Malivoire and Ryan Frieson
Original illustrations © Capstone Global Library 2010
Original illustration p.29 © Steve Walker
Illustrated by Mendola Ltd and Steve Walker
Picture research by Tracy Cummins
Production control by Victoria Fitzgerald
Originated by Capstone Global Library Ltd
Printed and bound in China by CTPS

ISBN 978 1 406216 19 6 (hardback)
14 13 12 11 10
10 9 8 7 6 5 4 3 2 1

ISBN 978 1 406216 24 0 (paperback)
15 14 13 12 11
10 9 8 7 6 5 4 3 2 1

British Library Cataloguing in Publication Data
Veitch, Catherine
Sea monsters. – (Legends of the sea)
001.9'44-dc22
A full catalogue record for this book is available from the
British Library.

Acknowledgements
We would like to thank the following for permission to
reproduce photographs: akg-images pp.**9** (© Peter Connolly),
25; Alamy p.**6** (© Adam Silver); AP Photo p.**19** (NZPA/Ross
Setford); Art Resource, NY p.**7** (Erich Lessing); Corbis p.**23**
(© Denis Scott); Getty Images p.**18** (Ministry of Fisheries);
istockphoto pp.**26 left** (© Philip Roop) **26 right** (© ido
hirshberg), **27** (© natsmith1); National Geographic Stock pp.**11,
20** (Minden Pictures/Norbert Wu), **13, 14** (Paul Sutherland);
Photolibrary p.**12** (Karen Gowlett-Holmes); Shutterstock
p.**15** (© Niar), **21** (© ampower); The Bridgeman Art Library
International p.**17** (Bibliotheque des Arts Decoratifs, Paris,
France / Archives Charmet).

We would like to thank Steve Walker for his invaluable help in
the preparation of this book.

Every effort has been made to contact copyright holders of
material reproduced in this book. Any omissions will be rectified
in subsequent printings if notice is given to the publishers.

Some words are shown in bold, **like this**. You can find
out what they mean by looking in the glossary.

Contents

Is it true?

Legends, or stories, have been told about strange creatures that live in the sea. Do you know which of these monsters are real and which are not?

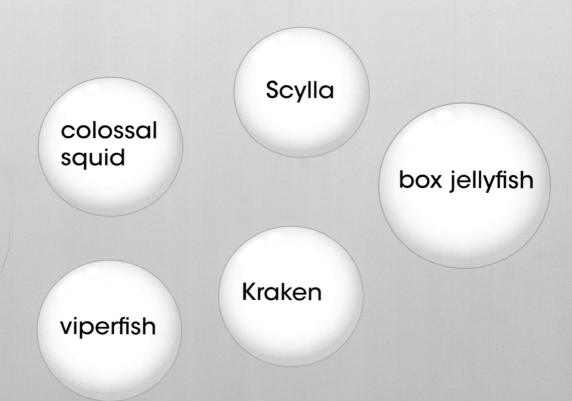

Scylla

colossal squid

box jellyfish

Kraken

viperfish

Read on to meet these sea monsters and others. Find out if you are right.

These signs will tell you if the sea monsters are real, not real, or if we don't know.

real   not real   don't know

In a spin

Long ago, people in Greece told stories of a sea monster called Charybdis [say "car-ib-dis"]. They say she created giant **whirlpools** by swallowing and burping up seawater.

In a whirlpool water swirls in a circle and can pull things under.

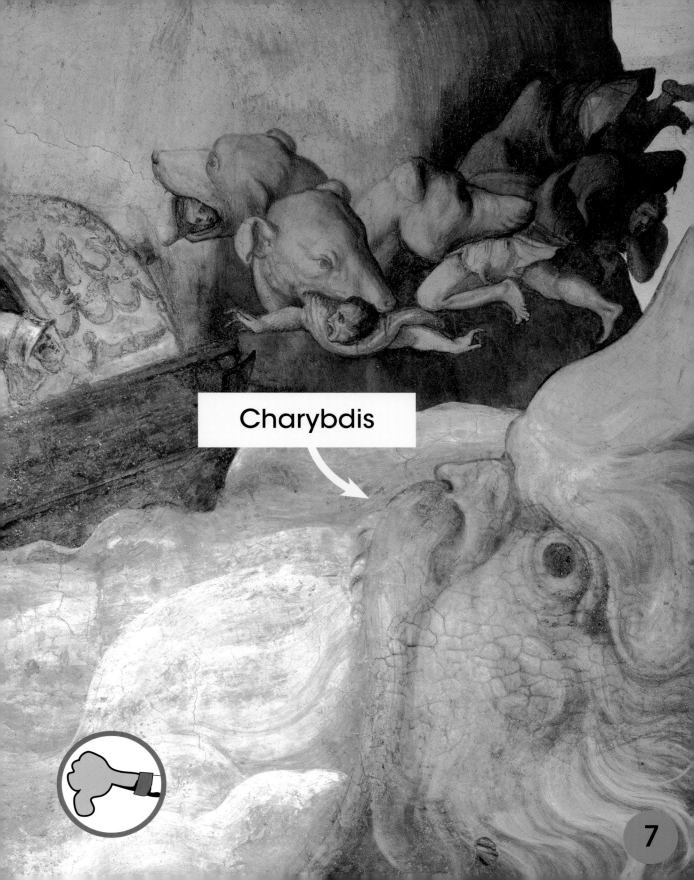

Charybdis

The monstrous sea goddess Scylla [say "sill-uh"] lived near Charybdis. Scylla had twelve dog's legs and six huge dog's heads. She had three rows of teeth in each head !

Some **legends** say that Scylla actually had six heads on snake-like necks.

Fierce fangs

The viperfish is only about 30 centimetres long. That's about as long as two pens put end to end. But it has fierce **fangs**, or teeth, that make this small fish extra scary.

fangs

The viperfish swims towards its **prey** at high speed and then attacks with its fangs.

prey

viperfish

IS IT TRUE?

The viperfish gets its name because it has a body and fangs like a viper snake.

Answer: true

11

Super stingers

Some types of box jellyfish are among the most **poisonous** creatures on Earth. Their name comes from their box shape. They have about 15 **tentacles** on each corner and each tentacle can have thousands of stinging cells!

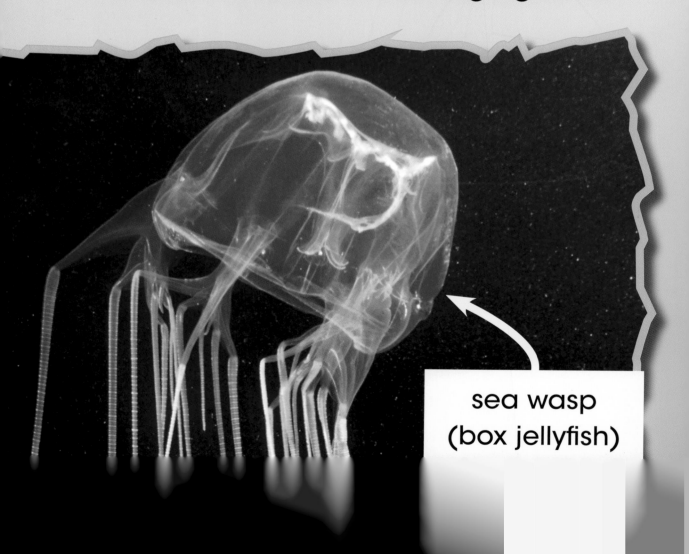

sea wasp
(box jellyfish)

IS IT TRUE?

The sea wasp is a deadly type of box jellyfish. It has enough poison to kill 60 people.

Answer: true

tentacle

13

Once stung by a sea wasp box jellyfish, you could have only minutes to live. Their stings are incredibly painful. **Victims** may die of a heart attack before even reaching land. People need to get help quickly to survive this scary attack!

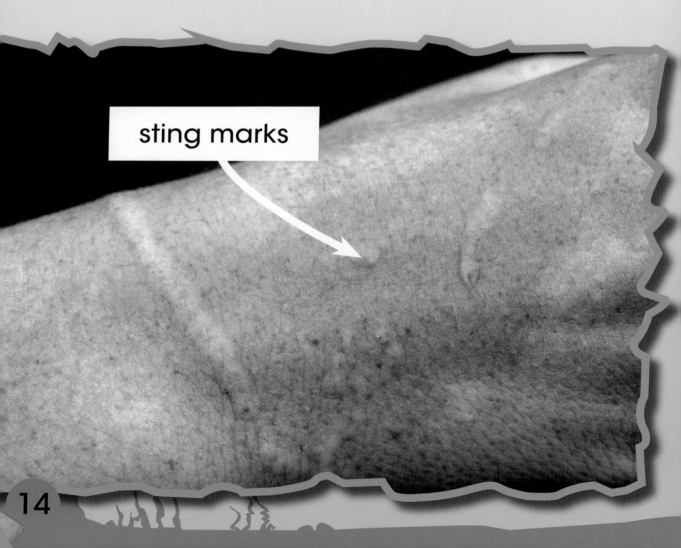

sting marks

vinegar

MARINE STINGERS
ARE PRESENT
IN THESE WATERS
DURING THE
SUMMER MONTHS

✚ VINEGAR
MARINE STINGS
DO NOT RUB
CAL ATTENTION

DID YOU KNOW?
Pouring vinegar over a
box jellyfish sting can
help to stop the **poison**.

15

Sirens' song

Some ancient Greek **legends** told the story of the Sirens. When sailors heard the Sirens' beautiful singing they could not turn away. They steered their ships towards the Sirens. Their ships were smashed to pieces on rocks.

The best way to survive a Siren's singing is to cover your ears!

Siren

Odysseus

DID YOU KNOW?

Legends say Odysseus heard the Sirens' song and lived. His men tied him up so that he couldn't steer the boat. Then they blocked up their ears.

Shy squid

A few years ago a colossal squid was caught near New Zealand. This giant squid weighed 495 kilograms. That's about as heavy as seven men! Only a few colossal squid have ever been found. None of these have been alive.

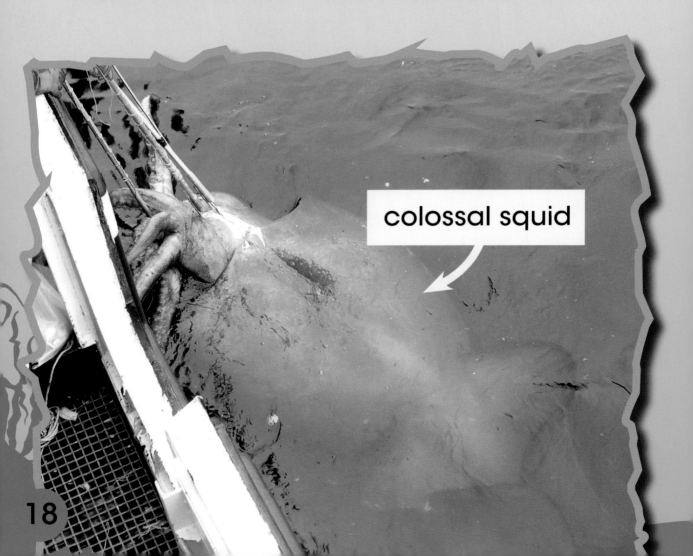

colossal squid

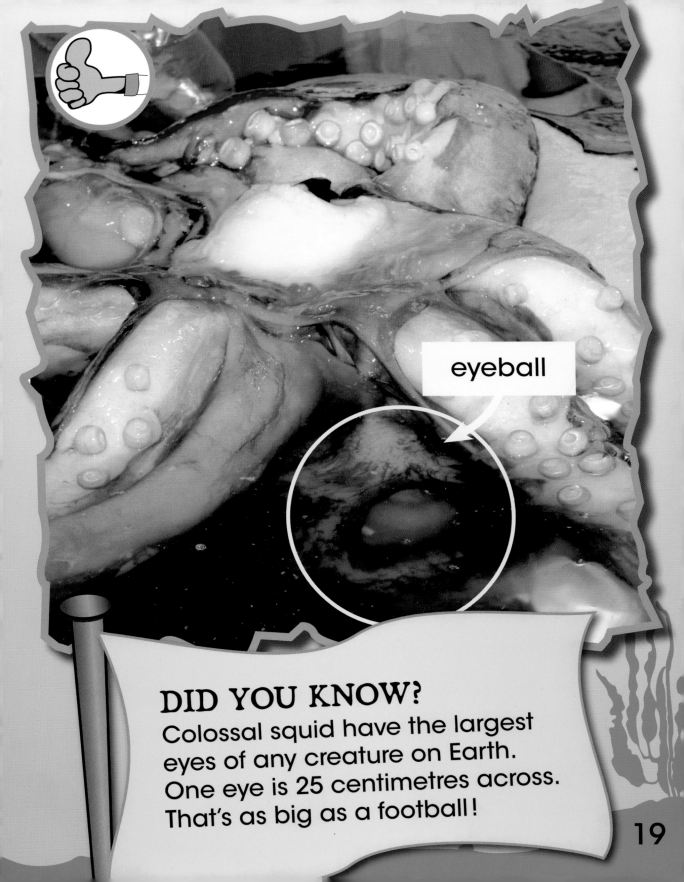

eyeball

DID YOU KNOW?

Colossal squid have the largest eyes of any creature on Earth. One eye is 25 centimetres across. That's as big as a football!

Greedy gulper

The gulper eel has a huge mouth. It can open its mouth wide enough to swallow **prey** much larger than itself. Prey are animals eaten by other animals. Its stomach can also stretch to fit in a bigger meal!

The gulper eel has a light at the end of its whip-like tail, which attracts prey towards its mouth.

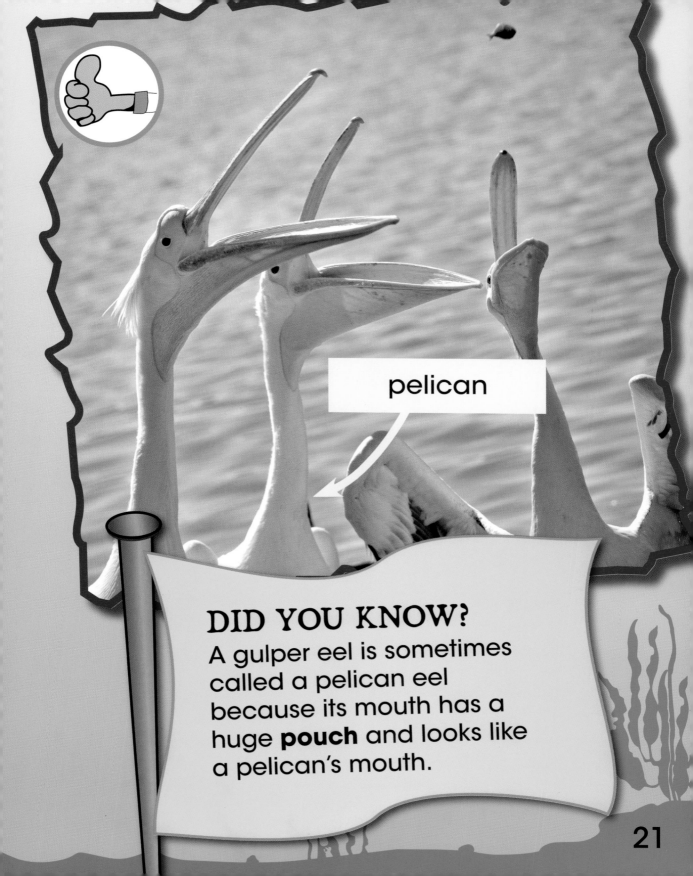

pelican

DID YOU KNOW?

A gulper eel is sometimes called a pelican eel because its mouth has a huge **pouch** and looks like a pelican's mouth.

Noisy neighbour

The blue whale is the loudest animal on Earth. It is even louder than an aeroplane. Its whistle can be heard under the ocean for many kilometres.

DID YOU KNOW?

The blue whale is the largest animal that ever lived. It grows to about 24 metres long. That's as long as two buses put end to end!

Crazy Kraken

Legends of the Kraken describe a sea monster that is so big that it is mistaken for an island. Some stories say that sailors who land on the Kraken are sucked underwater. Others say that the Kraken's huge **tentacles** drag whole ships underwater.

tentacle

DID YOU KNOW?
Some people think the Kraken is actually a colossal squid and that some of the stories about it may be true.

Monster hunters

People who study and search for **legendary** creatures are called **cryptozoologists** [say "crip-toe-zoo-ol-o-gists"]. Who knows what monsters lurk in the deep, dark depths of the world's oceans?

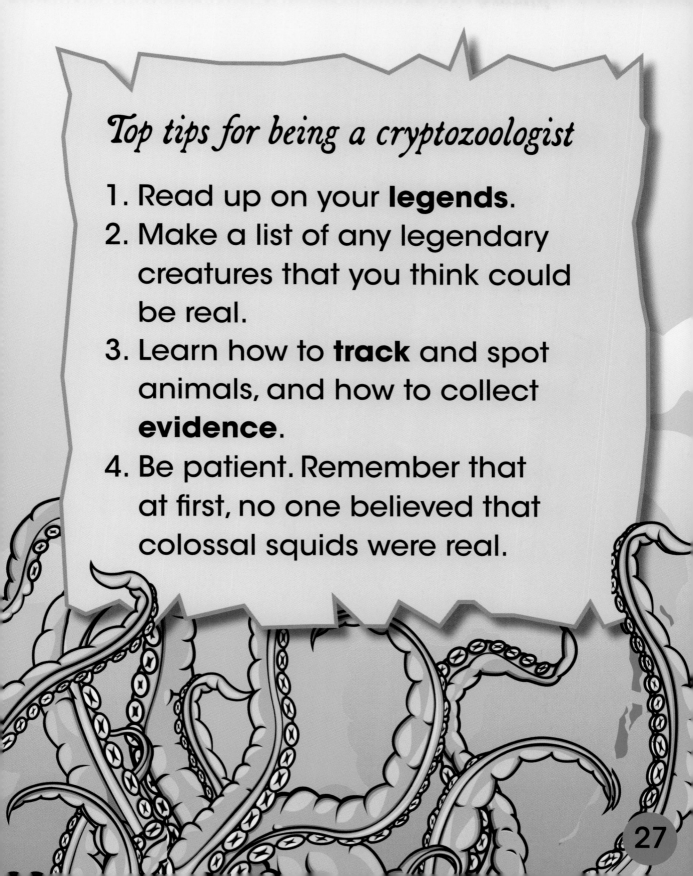

Top tips for being a cryptozoologist

1. Read up on your **legends**.
2. Make a list of any legendary creatures that you think could be real.
3. Learn how to **track** and spot animals, and how to collect **evidence**.
4. Be patient. Remember that at first, no one believed that colossal squids were real.

Imagine you are a **cryptozoologist** and come face-to-face with a sea monster. Draw what you imagine the monster would look like.

Make a table like this to help you plan your monster first. Use your imagination to fill out the columns.

Special features	Lives	Eats
large eyes, sharp teeth, three tentacles	under rocks	people

Give your monster a name.

Croctopus

Glossary

cryptozoologist person who investigates legendary or mystery creatures to find out if they are real or not

evidence information used to prove something

fangs sharp, pointed teeth

legend story that started long ago. Legends can be true or made up.

legendary something that comes from a legend

poisonous dangerous to humans or other animals. Poison can cause illness or death.

pouch part of an animal's body where things can be kept. It is similar to a pocket.

prey animals that are hunted and killed for food

tentacle long, thin part of a creature's body similar to an arm

track follow

victim person or group of people who are harmed

whirlpool place in the sea or a river where water swirls around in a circle. Sometimes whirlpools are strong enough to drag things under the water.

Find out more

Find out

Which creature has no heart?

Books

Animal Top Tens: The Oceans' Most Amazing Animals, Anita Ganeri (Raintree, 2008)

Sharks and Other Creatures From the Deep (Dorling Kindersley, 2008)

The World's Most Dangerous Animals, Paul Mason (Raintree, 2006)

Websites

atschool.eduweb.co.uk/carolrb/greek/greek1.html
Learn about ancient Greek sea monsters.

news.bbc.co.uk/cbbcnews/hi/pictures/galleries/newsid_3881000/3881353.stm
Find out interesting facts about jellyfish on this website.

www.seasky.org/deep-sea/deep-sea-menu.html
Take on the role of a deep sea explorer on this website. Click on the creatures you discover to find out more about them.

Index